New

C015423833

This book is due for return on or before the last date shown
above: it may, subject to the book not being reserved by
another reader, be renewed by personal application, post, or
telephone, quoting this date and details of the book.

HAMPSHIRE COUNTY COUNCIL 100%
County Library recycled paper

TSAR
Toronto
1997

We acknowledge the support of the Canada Council for the Arts for our publishing program. We also acknowledge support from the Ontario Arts Council.

Cover art and layout by Patricia Mackie Fee, inspired by the painting *Octobre* by James Tissot, c.1877, Musée des beaux-arts, Montreal.

Canadian Cataloguing in Publication Data

Thorpe, Michael
  Loves and other poems

ISBN 0-920661-64-5

I. Title.
PS8589.H67L68 1997   C811'.54   C97-931546-8
PR9199.3.T46L68 1997

Printed in Canada by Coach House Printing.

TSAR Publications
P. O. Box 6996, Station A
Toronto, Ontario M5W 1X7
Canada

For

Elin

and

Sathya

CONTENTS

I

Loves (I–XXII)

An Ongoing Sequence

I

His insistent memory
was of captive Sundays —
suited, collared, compelled
to keep his chair,
prolong his ice
with cautious licks.

She had sat, meanwhile,
erect, sipping demitasses,
smoke leaking from her nostrils —
hardly moved, unless
he threatened to edge
from his chair and stray.
She seized him then,
placed him firmly back.

Only years after did he learn
where father was those days,
that unloving man
with a hateful woman
for whom at last he left:
when she thought him old enough
to learn, he would atone
by fidelity to the one true
woman he believed he knew.

II

After many years, only mother
and daughter, unmarried, remained;
sometimes the mother pondered —
studying that undesired flesh —
she should have had a man
(who may at least leave one
the best of daughters),
while the daughter reflected
how, since father died,
mother has become herself —
if they could go on so forever . . .
The mother dying, she turned
sharp and odd, friendless;
all agreed she needed a man,
but in truth she was simply alone.

III

She feels there's nothing they cannot share
or speak of: they stroll, like sisters,
hand in arm; they are the envy
of all who watch them pass —
their closeness would have endured lifelong,
finer than her loved men's grasp,
had her daughter only been born.

IV

Call this number, he said,
and you will hear her voice:
"This is Greta, I cannot come
to the phone just now but leave
a message, I will return your . . ."
She had in fact been dead
six months past and they'd lived
apart years before she died;
it had worked better so,
their life together was hateful,
apart unbroken romance,
every call an assignation.
Now he would make it last,
still rented that space wherein
her voice held vacant possession.

V

"With her he was so alive:
I spied on them together
across a dark café; he smiled
often, talked to make her laugh,
or bent his head attentive.
She wore a slit skirt and once
when it slipped, baring her thigh,
he reached across like one
possessing and possessed,
to cover it. I glimpsed then
the broad gold band
I placed there and felt it,
as he caressed her flesh,
                    burn mine."

VI

Her plea, "You do love me?"
told him he did not —
at that moment she felt it,
a dank breath in a dark alley —
though he only said, "Don't be silly"
and they kissed. Never again
did she seek such reassurance,
while he would often claim:
"She and I have never
been ones to say much."

VII

"I can't," she breathed, "live without you":
at those words his mind clouded,
their future was foreclosed:
he reached across, squeezed her wrist,
moved a strand of hair
from the corner of an anxious eye.
He felt in life the oppression
of his absence, as if to die
would be faithless desertion,
while still she waited for a word —
"Don't speak so, you must go on,"
he murmured. But why?
Neither dared voice that question.

VIII

In Harunobu's print a couple portray
communion of art and desire:
he reclines, quietly lodged in her,
buffing his nails;
she, robe hitched high, balances upon
his unassertive penis,
drawing a tune from a mandolin;
three volumes of verse
lie ready at his elbow:
next, he will recite
while she remains sweetly impaled.

It all occurs *en plein air*
framed by gentle leaning trees
and a flimsy dwelling
that never knew the winds:
surely, no one sees
who does not envy this.

(Suzuki Harunobu, 1725?–1770; Ny Carlesberg Glyptotek,
Copenhagen)

IX

TISSOT'S "OCTOBER" (1877)
A PORTRAIT OF MRS KATHLEEN NEWTON (d. 1882)

Clutching her rouched purple skirts
clear of neat black button boots
and a rustling patch of petticoats,
she stoops under autumn's chestnuts,
      casts back in ambush
      of her hat's black wheel
      a glance of dominant charm:
so his mind's brush often held her
as she turned back to Newton —
the book warm beneath her arm
an alibi for absence, an outing
to the library for some new romance.

Did Tissot foresee his bright girl's
early fall? His painting calls
after, through gravity-struck leaves.

(Musée des beaux-arts, Montréal)

X

All said, they could not grasp
what she sees in him, he in her—
that was the beauty of it,
each knew from the start
it was them against the world—
nothing less would suffice.

XI

LOOKIN' FOR LOVE

Witty successful vibrant attractive
mid-forties non-smoking vegetarian
cat lover enjoys concerts walks travel
seeks unattached distinguished gentleman
for caring compatible fun while we live . . .

Though the room darkens daily,
there's light enough yet to create
a commercial for the desirable self,
a hopeful *carpe diem* for the Personals.

XII

Surely you have realized I love you?
There must be something we can do.
My husband is a good man,
faithful but so dull, dead really;
I could live again with you.

It's strange, he said, my wife and I
have sometimes imagined I or she
might undertake a compassionate affair,
that we might from the much we have
spare some love for another in need.

I can't believe you have said this—
that you could treat my love as a case
you would return home and discuss,
your fingers reeking of my sex,
in tones of atrocious pity?

(She then flung out, her love reviled).

Trembling, he sat on and regretted
how, in fear of what she offered,
he had repulsed her with a pretence
of abundant marital happiness—
though he knew all too well what she suffered.

XIII

There's no fool, they sneer, like an old one:
she breathes, He's so attentive, he worships me;
the young men call it an abuse of flesh
and leer at the little digger for gold —
but they when she crosses hissing thighs
intensely stare.
          He, contented, sighs:
she's just what I've wanted all my life,
I know she loves me for myself . . .

XIV

He asked, Would she be kind?
He felt so young, still vital,
but his wife was a cripple—
and was she too not alone?

They need not lie about love,
pretend to more than need—
mutual, he felt sure—
but for her it was less simple:

Though he was gentle,
considerate, pressed no claim,
her flesh could not collaborate
with her softened heart,
to embrace yet stay compassionate.

XV

Their love spurned privacy:
they came and went freely,
shared, even, relief of nature—
would piss and shit
in each other's sight.

This was, if not entirely
beautiful, open
truthful odorous—
and, yes, exciting:
they by this metaphor
embraced utter being.

XVI

GAY EVENING

Idly they debated beforehand
which one would be wife,
but the evening made no excuse
for such poor relief.
The younger neither minced
nor played coquette;
the older, more frankly affectionate,
needed now and then to brush
the half-bare arm he must have known
he could not claim for very long.

They banished, as they talked, lies
their minds had brought:
offered, with rarely warm goodbyes
veiled amends for vulgar thought.

XVII

They said it was only pity
that clutched him to her—
her beauty sunk beneath
incised waves of pain—
but almost daily he assured her
she was her first self in his eyes:
it could not be otherwise,
or he would have become less
than the man he believed in,
loving her to death . . .

XVIII

He rose from the bed,
potent, fulfilled,
but she lay still and said
within it was nothing;
her body chilled,
she watched from the dead
as he shrugged clothes back on
with his air of a job well done,
yet he had only served himself
when he drove his piston home
and cried for himself alone . . .

Though she could have cried for that,
not for any joy he gave her,
she did call out instead
at the instant she judged right
so he should again be misled.

XIX

He could not imagine he was old:
it was always his young self he saw
approaching them, and he would talk
as if all life lay ahead and they
would be a treasured part of it.

They saw, in their astonishment,
a collapsed, faded being, absurdly
draped in crisp, meticulous clothing
mouthing with flecked unconscious
saliva his deathless devotion —

they saw he could not imagine he was old.

XX

Women spoke of him as considerate,
gentle, and wove pleasing rumours
of an early unrequited love —
or else he must have surely been
that perfect husband none had known:
what less could explain his single state?

The trick was, he feared them all,
loathed their dangling breasts
and the hairy triangle he once glimpsed
even the mother who loved him possessed:
so, while in thought they embraced him
his chivalrous hatred evaded their touch.

15

XXI

TERMINAL

Once she knew his sickness was terminal,
she began looking forward to looking back,
made up her tale of happiness they'd shared:
impatient to tell it, as he too slowly died,
she betrayed by withdrawal she'd never cared
for the drugged fearful man, hollow-eyed—

Who saw, as she sat by with forced concern,
he had outlived her professed devotion,
but even as he died he could still
with his eyes' mute reproach spoil
the posthumous pretence she had prepared.

XXII

"HOME"

After all, their distinct lives had led
to this scrupulously ordered place
where cheerful brisk women polished
their abraded flesh and young gardeners
hemmed them in with keen roses . . .

And where, confiding strangers,
they in carefree intervals traded
reconstructions of vanished beings
framed in salvaged photographs, whom
they had loved or sought to love . . .

Though a few bitterly lapsed,
most clung to doting anecdote,
so that it seemed, removed from life,
love was born of afterthought.

II

Trapped Light

A Sequence

He knew that there was no sky . . .
it was only light which had been trapped

PETER ACKROYD, *First Light*

For
Edmund, Jacob & Lucy

1. KODAKED

A rare snapshot trapped him
in pushchair pouting aside
from a grinning hand:
though his mature relations
never approached perfection
he laughed off all connection
with the fastidious animal
that arch image seemed to expose.

2. EXPEDITION 1

A walk to the beach
enveloped in sun, only
one such early day recalled,
playing safe in the aura
of the mother's soft shade.

3. CONTINGENT

The shore did not expect him —
he displaced pebbles,
scuffed some sand
and left it
unmoved.

21

4. EXCURSION

Once only
   on the steamer *Belle*
Once only
   to view the seals
      and inhale
the rails' briny varnish.
  Little else distils —
only a sense of Sunday self
  in exalted progress
  outpacing the quays —
   then, returning,
  subject to their arrest.

5. BESIDE THE SEA

Hold to the straining ear
shells of the seaside cottage, hear
clattering laughter of board games,
but they say it always rained —
smothering sky, dishwater sea —
he agitating to return to the dark
of that yardless back-to-back.

6. EXPEDITION 2

Approaching grandfather meant terror
of the corridorless carriage,
dreading the panicky wrenching
at the window strap, unbelieving
in the certain saving face
and the handle firmly turned:
they would walk up after tea
to feed the immense pig swedes
until once it was gone, "sold" —
innocent of its untold slaughter,
he dreamt only
of his homeward frenzied journey.

7. EXPEDITION 3

Clinging to the roped stack
he stared down upon
the damp undulating field
of the horse's enormous back,
fear courage risk knotted,
jolted in the abrupt ruts
of his ninth dry summer.

8. EXPEDITION 4:

White House and Smithy

To spy the great white house
in a green fold of earth
he walked and ran far
beyond permitted limits,
pathless in Africa . . .
But did return, at twilight,
and fighting his heart
peered through the last hedge
at village edge,
saw the humped red-eyed smithy
erupt —then at its clanking din
fled home as from a Judgement.

9. WAITING

He seems always waiting
in the bleak narrow street
after the forgotten film, bound
home one night of many,
neither understanding nor understood—
and waits there still.

10. CHRISTMAS ORANGES

"Heroes of the Merchant Navy"
was his first School Prize—
a careful inspiring choice
in 'forty-three, but its very
title repelled: so it sank
unread—perhaps to surface
in some distant jumble sale
and still somewhere linger,
foxed and brittle, with grainy
photographs of strained faces
that threading U-boat packs
had landed Christmas oranges
he thoughtlessly sucked dry.

11. LIMELIGHT

Bernie Simmons, the name returns,
a widowed mother pressing clothes,
little more, only
they were best friends; suddenly
Bernie died and made him important.

There was solemn service at school,
sidelong glances his way:
they felt high for days,
being about twelve
and compliant with time.

12. LESSON

"You know nothing":
the boys sat arms folded
stilled by some lurking truth—
that the ivory-skinned aged
young teacher of French
had known in Japanese captivity;
their resentment smouldered,
of his superior torment.

13. COMMUNION CLASS

The decent vicar, eyes averted,
tendered his charts of heaven and hell;
the crass immortal boys
pedalled away from his gate,
their laughter across the marsh
volleyed in his vacillating study.

14. "THE REGAL"

He approached by crimson stairs
brass rods ruled, observed
from plush imperial seats
his youth's myths of nobly
diffident heroics—from
In Which We Serve to *Shane*:
after, those stairs seemed stained,
a flaying wind trawled
from the sea that swallowed
Leslie Howard—but *Shane* remained,
purely other, with Hershey bars,
Wrigley's and laconic tailored GIs.

15. STRIDER

Winter-striding the seawall
between detonating waves,
he imagined he could straddle
all immune from sheer force:
only then, for some years, could he
so insouciantly dodge winter's sea.

16. COMING IN LATE

Creeping in, after the last bus,
he would hear, "Is that you?"
and retort, "No, it's me!"

Now, the buses no longer run,
her voice is never heard,
new families chant their lines.

17. LOSS

At his mother's death he suddenly saw
that none then remained to embroider
fond tales of his winning childhood.

III

Eight Poems

for

THOMAS HARDY

THE HARDY SOCIETY VISITS MAX GATE

Self-drawn to declare the substance
won by a "good hand at a serial,"
stark at first, with time a lichened,
tree-hemmed pile—no new-thatched
vision of cramped Bockhampton:

We gossip as if he were family,
pick over our Tom's contradictions:
the faithless church-haunting
celebrant of rustic worth,
the ridiculed Hodge's champion
who craved the London season
to snuffle at the decolletages
of perfectly useless noble dames . . .

"When did he and Emma stop
sharing a bed: why no children,
they seem to have wanted them—
and did he meanly deny Florence
a bath?" "I can feel," murmurs
a woman deeply involved,
"the unhappiness here . . ."

Here Emma kept chickens,
here the side gate they say
he escaped unwanted callers by;
here, shaded, among ground ivy
the endearing pets' cemetery,
inscriptions carved, in his Jude
persona, by the master—
Wessex, as ever to the fore,
"Faithful, Unflinching."

Was his own final syllable "Em"?

— beyond elegy and blame
half her name?

Such trivia, Hardy would see,
align the Wizard with this humanity
that breaches, posthumously,
his life's long privacy—
the bypass beats at the window
where Tess and Jude were born;
as to rear his ponderous villa
Roman bones were torn from rest,
so he knew we'd scuff at his dust;
aftercomers will have his heart.

(July 1992)

BEAUTY AMONG THE TURNIPS

"But these women! If out into rough wrappers in
a turnip-field, where would their beauty be?"
                        HARDY, *Notebook*, March 15, 1890

> How, he mused, would his London ladies fare
> bent in a turnip field at turn of the year:
> it seems a perverse notion to occur
> to one so besotted with their beauty—
>   or did the writer thus in fancy
>   violate what the starved man
> yearned for across the brilliant table?

A FANCY WOMAN FOR HARDY

(Suggested by Alfred Stevens's *A First Night
at the Palace Theatre*)[1]

Prudent scholarship declines speculation—
no fleshly mistress for Emma-free Hardy,
even one night in naughty nineties London
is denied his balding bowed head—
the woman's merely there to prettify the scene.

Let us instead suppose that bold Hardy
cheats doubly on Sue-hating Emma
and that proper tease Mrs Henniker
(whom he took to *The Master Builder*)
with his creamy-bosomed neighbour—
who turns languorously toward us
insinuating what he discreetly conceals:
    that they come freshly sated
    from a stolen bed or will share it
    after roaring in the stalls
    at the hair-down music hall.

1. c. 1900, including Hardy, Conrad and unidentified glamorous
women.

HARDY AND DR MARIE

" . . . it is not improbabilities of incident but improbabilities of character
that matter," HARDY, *Life*, 1886

Dr Marie Stopes campaigned for birth control
from her phallic dwelling on Portland Bill:
Hardy twice her age visited her there,
told her plain that her play *Vectia*—
denied a licence to perform—was worse
than immoral, improbable—no wife
of three years could remain so ignorant
of "physiology, especially with a young man
just through the party-wall ready to teach her."
Things equally odd occurred in *Jude*
thirty years before, but to remind one
so revered of improbabilities
he'd committed would have seemed merely rude.

HARDY AND THE OTHER ANIMALS

Impartial Hardy endowed
a starveling thrush with soul—
equated with the nightingale—
hawk and hedgehog upon their trails
were mysteries; a blinded bird
the quintessence of *caritas* . . .

Such claims may seem absurd:
what thrush or bird forgives the worm?
The hawk's out to rend the dewfall shrew—
most, like men, are hunters
and thrive on random slaughters.

This Hodge-descended Hardy saw:
knew between "higher" and "lower"
difference only—not of soul,
but crass human presumption,
as when Fanny's black Samaritan
is stoned from the workhouse door.

THOMAS HARDY AND THE LION

Thomas Hardy mused in '03
that if lions had enjoyed
our evolutionary luck
they would now be kinder than we:

We who say he fights like a lion,
is lion-hearted, leonine,
swear by maned symbols
of majesty and justice . . .

Hardy mocking all such parallels
returned the lion to itself
and exposed man by his hyperbole
as true king of bestiality.

HARDY'S MODEST PROPOSAL

To the Revd S Whittell Key

Hardy with harsh compassion
put it to a clergyman
agitated about blood sports
and their degrees of pain
that one might utilise
for the shoot surplus children,
so delivering them from lives
less happy than animals' or birds'.

ALAS, POOR HIGNETT!

Where, wrote Hignett to Great Hardy,
a month before he would die
gnarled with honoured years,
may I place my fiction of sixty
thousand words and these verses?
Only, vouchsafed the Name
"with thanks" by submitting
your MS to a suitable publisher
and asking his terms: fair
but frosted words. Alas,
Hardy's editors note,
no works of Hignett
ever achieved print—

Poor Hignett, yet that name,
forever enambered in Hardy's reply,
will cling to his gleaned Remains.

IV

Ordinary Men

ORDINARY MEN

"Evil that arises out of ordinary thinking and is committed by ordinary
people is the norm, not the exception."

> ERVIN STAUB, *The Roots of Evil: the Origins of Genocide
> and Other Group Violence.*

"If the men of Reserve Police Battalion 101 could become killers under
such circumstances, what group of men cannot?"

> CHRISTOPHER R BROWNING, final sentence of
> *Ordinary Men: Reserve Police Battalion 101
> & the Final Solution in Poland.*

Their beginnings were almost innocuous:
escorting Jews for—in official
euphemistic jargon—"resettlement"
in the East was a lifetime's break,
for these ordinary middle-aged men—
dockers, truckers, salesmen, clerks—
to see a bit of the world beyond
Hamburg, and so they came to Poland . . .

When they gathered near Jósefów
in a cool midsummer's dawn,
it was, stated SS Captain Wohlauf,
for "an extremely interesting task,"
a "special action," 1500 Jews
to be disposed of that day—
serviceable men to be selected
for labour, their women, children,
the frail and old to be shot.
The Captain expected no cowards.
But their commander, Major Wilhelm Trapp,
fifty-three, unfit for the SS
though he bore an Iron Cross,
whom the men fondly called Papa,
took a less absolute view.
When he mustered and addressed

them near the sleeping village,
he invited older men who felt
unequal to the task to step out:
only Otto Julius Schimke did,
but then ten or a dozen more
surrendered rifles and awaited
assignment to milder duties—
guarding the driven Jews
or trucking them to the woods—
who had more courage then,
those who kept ranks
or those who declined?

Why did a mere dozen abstain?
Some perhaps hesitated, uncertain
if they qualified for Trapp's exemption;
whatever stumbling words he found,
hindsight suggests he had himself in mind.

Among Trapp's officers one,
Buchmann, a merchant
of some refinement,
refused such demeaning work.

Those things would be hard to do,
even though only to Jews.
Some practised personal forms
of selective mitigation—
would not shoot infants or
small children, or fired
deliberately wide, left the killing
to harder or more fearful colleagues;
a former metalworker rationalized,
assuming the mothers must be shot,
that he would kill *only* children,
to release them—"erlösen,"
which means also to redeem—
from a motherless fate . . .

Even the steeliest became sickened
at the killing ground: neck shots,
as prescribed, were seldom neat—
parts of their targets flew
and vomiting shooters stumbled off,
green uniforms besmirched
with blood, brains, shards of bone—
but if some could not go on, most
stuck it out and were strong.

Throughout that day Major Trapp
kept apart, an absent father:
leaving the business to devoted
young officers, he paced or slumped
in the village schoolroom weeping,
a weak, demoralising commander—
but was at day's end granted
some relief, in the apparition
of a girl survivor brought
to him, bleeding from the head:
taking her in his arms, he said
"You shall remain alive," and so
his sentimentality was assuaged.

Such was their "interesting" initiation.
Later massacres disturbed less—
but mostly, in mass deportations,
while in roundups they still
shot the old and frail, Trapp ruled
that was their utmost duty,
they should not beat or torture;
their main job became to stock
the ghettoes for onward dispatch
to "some sort of camp" where the real
killing was less personally done—
most zealous was Lieutenant Gnade,
in normal life a forwarding agent . . .

But even the queasy Trapp

43

could by September efficiently conduct
reprisal killings of Poles and Jews,
discounted at two hundred to one—
once even fastidious Buchmann
could not evade the kill—
few could now, though there had
always been shooters enough.
                    By Miedzyrzec,
Germanized by some to the simpler
Menschendreck ('human horror')
all understood about destinations,
even the Jews who as they tramped,
stripped of every possession,
sang "We are travelling to Treblinka"
(*they* did not march to see the world).

Weaker feelings were shovelled deep:
some noted Captain Hoffmann's disabling
dysentery coincided with roundups,
while a hardier type could boast
he needed his bag of Jews
before breakfast—yet there were few,
it seems, raw bloodthirst drove,
their need rather to be held,
in steeled readiness to kill, men . . .

All shared Trapp's outspoken shame
when young SS Captain Wohlauf,
his deputy, brought a young bride
to witness the "Menschendreck" roundup:
such sights were unfit for German women.

Their last massacre, at Lublin,
in the final fall of '43,
was dubbed the Harvest Festival:
mostly they goaded and guarded,
ensured an orderly procession
of targets for the specialists.
When it ended, those five hundred

commonplace policemen had dealt
or facilitated the extinction
of eighty-three thousand Jews,
a modest routine contribution
to Himmler's Final Solution . . .

In the muddled aftermath
most escaped retribution,
some became again mere policemen—
nor were there heroes, only
a certain tattered decency:
if Schimke, Bittner, nameless others
evaded killing, they oiled the machine;
they were not good, but weak.
Papa Trapp alone was hanged,
who at Jósefów had wept
"God have mercy on us Germans":
he died for them all at last,
one who in murdering his weaker self
proved a leader of ordinary men.

Note: As required by German privacy laws, most names used here
are pseudonyms, except those of Trapp, Wohlauf, Hoffmann and
Gnade, which "appear in other documentation in archives outside
Germany" (Browning, p. x).

(May–June '94)

V

Art, Politics,

Other Loves

LANDFALL, 1492

The Plaint of Juan Rodriguez Bermejo

"It was October 12, early morn,
I leant out from the rigging
of the *Pinta* and cried *Tierra!*
                    Tierra!
So, I have since been told
began an *otro mundo*, a New World—
but mark this, it rankles with me
still, I deserved for my first shout
those rewards our Sovereigns vowed,
a silk doublet and 10000 maravedis,
a year's wages for life—yet our
Admiral Colon claimed the lot
for some lights he said he saw
the evening before . . .
                    Take my word,
that's how it really began,
in the old and future fashion,
with a brass-faced cheat of the working-man."

MOCK EXECUTION OF A FRENCH RÉSISTANT (1944)

At the sun-filled angle of two walls,
head slightly bowed,
eyes shadowed,
forehead high, white,
he seems smiling;
hands out of sight
pinned back, chest narrow,
bared, he waits at ease.

Ranked between us and him,
the German firing squad takes aim,
awaits its officer's word,
who stands, neck open for the heat,
fists at belted waist,
seems weighing his powered moment
to remove the other from the sun.

The word "Fire!" never came:
they only meant to make him speak,
but whether he did so or not
he would disappear in a camp,
nothing left but this snapshot
in a dead German officer's pocket,
grinning on in careless undress
at the murderous charade.

(The Illustrated London News,
'Victory 45' Number, May 1995)

50

TWO POEMS FOR MILAN KUNDERA

LONG LIVE . . . !

(A Czech Anecdote)

When the Soviet puppet Husak
stood in '68
>   before the malleable young
>   they began to shout
>   Long Live Husak!
>   Long Live the Party!
He waited—
>   only, they did not stop:
red-faced, outfaced,
speechless, he left.
Thus with powerless might,
the Spirit of Schweik,
they returned upon him
the craven chant the falsely
accused had mouthed in '51:

Though no grand ironic shout
can quicken now
their laboured shuffle of freedom,
surely some who voiced it then
already knew their lives complete.

(1992)

KUNDERA'S "BLACK FLOWER"

In his novel "Immortality"
Kundera digresses briefly
to illustrate how fragile life
may interrupt immortal art:
a news report of a girl
who seeking suicide crouched
in the path of oncoming cars—
these, frantically avoiding her,
crashed in the ditch from which
arose screams of the injured—
and some were killed, but not she
who denied her death rose
and slipped away.
        After this news
the author returned reluctant
to his desk, bowed beneath
death's onrushing motor, yet
still he wrote and slipped away . . .

AUSTRIAN SABBATH

At the Romantik Park Hotel
an archduke bows you in to breakfast;
decently Sunday's burghers stroll
steady toward the bells, greet
their kind with ceremonious smiles:
an orderly place, almost homogeneous—
though trams in English celebrate
Coca-Cola: "You can't beat the feeling!"
and more passionately a muralist
    urges "Auslander Raus!"
    Yet few are visible,
    patient on their heels,
    hat inverted for coins
    at side doors of churches—
they may, one sees, disturb.

Trip out, then, to the Open Air Museum:
it seems to resolve confusion—
musicians in flowered braces
press the buoyant accordion,
strata of cold cuts are levelled,
white-socked children play with decorum.
Strolling round this charmed settlement,
    timbers redolent of toil,
    worship, due festivity,
one imagines a past sufficient,
    separate from history:
in a *Waldviertler* farmstead
the Crucified Christ leans over
    the living-room corner,
Holy Maria the conjugal bed;
    the One Book spread
    where best light falls.

(Graz, 1993)

53

READING *KING LEAR*
AT MIAMI INTERNATIONAL AIRPORT

(During the Presidential Campaign, 1992)

Man — and to be correct woman —
are utterly accommodated here:
pelican daughters are benign
muses of the Miami Restaurant's
mural, overseeing the earthly city
in pristine washed relief;
Nature is a kitsch goddess
in plastic or Teeshirted image,
Surfing is the body's scripture.

At intervals an emollient voice
welcomes a train of paying guests,
alligators grin a taste for fudge
Florida style; cooperative marlins
leap for mechanised fishermen,
Coca Cola Bopping Bottles sway . . .

This all seems beside the point of *Lear*
so I turn to *The Atlantic Monthly*
piqued by its question,
"Can George Bush Think?"
                    Could the old King?

Neither might be called reflective,
each has "but slenderly known himself":
      so kind a father,
      such family values . . .

At Miami Airport nothing less
than *Lear* blinds belief.

THOUGHTS WHILE INVIGILATING
A FIRST-YEAR ENGLISH FINAL, APRIL 1994

"The poetic act changes with the amount of background reality
embraced . . ."   CZESLAW MILOSZ

Bound to a three hours' wheel
they frown under interrogation
upon our relations
with 'God,' nature, ourselves . . .

Meanwhile, in Rwanda blue-helmeted men
like us look on
as a pleading woman is dragged past
by a machete-wielding killer:
their mandate forbids them to intervene.

How then can we at our desks,
poet or reader, claim to embrace
the dictum of Milosz, Warsaw survivor,
and not merely embellish
atrocity with words?

How really include the Rwandan woman
in what we see, think and feel?
This is the question
that grates the wheel.

EXOTIC

At my shoulder a padding camel
in a gritty nameless Turkish town
forty years back: winnowed memory.
Less willingly remembered: how
barefoot boys spat in the dust
at the foreigner's heel, or
reduced by Anatolian winter
clawed, still barefoot, for coin
flung from the hissing train.

REMEMBERING SAM

You were one who would always die too young;
your hybrid features bloomed beyond extremes—
in your presence one could feel relieved
of race, an impossible being
neither victor nor victim: that Sam was
your gift beyond explication or analysis,
beyond study or imitation, yourself.

(Sam Selvon, 1923–94)

TO WILSON HARRIS

(On his lecture before the Mysore Literary Society)

Your face equine, long wisdom,
Eyes shuttered, then a gleam
As you declaim the need of magic
In the world of modern fiction
Lest the world of modern fact
Come down upon our backs;

Before us excess *gulab jamun*
Congeals in syrup; below us
Rises Mysore streets' acrid cry
Greeting your voice of integrity
With history's indifferent no—
Or so I hear through my blind eyes

That glimpse beyond the saris
Of the cosseted beautiful women,
The nourished bulk of their men,
No signals from that deep voyage
On which your vision is compelled,
Only a mask of enduring hell . . .

But the last word should not be mine:
Passion like yours will move
If moving may be done,
Here or there transform one—
Decode across fouled streets of time
Words that free our nameless mime.

(May 1978)

BLAMELESS NASKAPI MAGIC

I

Wife, I dreamed tonight
of patterns for my coat,
that when I go out to hunt
caribou will accept death
at my hands; the soul-spirit
drew these shapes in my mind
that so clad I may kill without blame.

II

Husband, I will paint your coat
that when you shoot your prey
the spirit will preserve you
from resentment of the caribou:
so all will work as it should,
you will bring the blessed meat
that bloods my adorning hand.

The Museum of Newfoundland & Labrador

LIVINGSTONE'S POODLE

(d. January 15, 1867)

Imagine this small explorer
busying his days
in the heart of Africa
dashing and wagging
ahead and around the sweating column;
at every village he saw off
thieving mongrel monsters:
Livingstone, who neglected kindred
and quarrelled with his race
loved this "spirited little beast"
bought like any slave at Zanzibar.

Little else is known, only
that day as they floundered through
yet another swamp of waist-high water
Chitané, swimming beyond his strength
sank, forgotten—
yet perhaps he alone
of that dubious expedition
fulfilled his being's mission.

A SUNSET WALK OVER RED HILLS

"Where I was born and where and how I have lived is unimportant. It is
what I have done with where I have been that should be of interest."
GEORGIA O'KEEFFE

The black dog ahead of its mistress
in their eternal shared existence
turns a snapped instant
for assurance that she follows:
in this recurrent endless moment
in the lives of dogs and humans
she is a figure upon the canvas
of a subject she only inhabited,
the sensational canine world.

> (on a photograph by
> John Loengard, in *Life*, late 1960s)

LAWREN HARRIS'S
ATHABASCA VALLEY, JASPER

Expressing soul claims the catalogue—
and what is that but creating it?
In a single shattered tree
that like a broken dart
centres Athabasca's peaks—
that old Romantic image,
the single suffering tree,
stubborn tree
foregrounded . . .
Consigned to middle distance
smooth complete firs
cannot compete, none worthy

to stand alone and apart:
only a broken shaft
fits a sense of soul.
So, standing before
hard mountains' bland backdrop,
we find soul-self in wood
splintered by time and frost.

(Owens Art Gallery, 1992)

CHOU CH'I ACCEPTS A COMMISSION

Esteemed patron: I well understand
what it is you desire
as a gift for your friend—
two persistent pines
burnished in winter's fires.

I have explored in old books
beyond a common dauber's ken
and know that while I paint
to gratify a client's ideal
I delineate only my soul—
which over and over again I sell,
yet remain a poor man
tenacious as cedar or pine.

Note: no painting by Chou Ch'i is known
to have survived (James Cahill)

RAINBOW OVER EXETER:
A CONSTRUCTED IMAGE

For Thaddeus Holownia

A sudden rainbow springs from sullen grey,
But few look up and none pause to gaze at
An explicable arrangement of reflected light,
No heavenly covenant with a blessed city;
Lucky we happened here camera-slung:
Snared in that square the scene may hatch
Mystery— but for dark crowd-blobs that cling
To Exe Bridge beneath the glowing arch;
Impossible in this secular composition
To shift the squat Cathedral central—
Quick! superimpose that snapped flight of swans
Caught thrumming downriver one casual
Day, make them burr like immortal engines
Between the rainbow's never-fading portals.

TAKEN UNAWARES

He would often rehearse a good death:
    with brave parting smile,
    a firm agnostic refusal
    of anodyne illusion—
    perhaps a wry grimace
    of resignation; but what
    he had never prepared
    was the heart's sharp stop,
    alone and untended
just as the days' light was lengthening.

62

THE YORK VENUS (1869)

Albert Moore's heavy-legged Venus
    with shaven fissureless
    mound and hairless armpits,
    breasts that fail to lift
    with the lifted arm,
    has the head and torso
    of a Greek *kouros* . . .

This varies the classic topic
of the Victorian veiled erotic:
Albert's Venus beneath the lines
is Apollo in drag of female flesh.

                                (York City Art Gallery)

SEX AND THE LOTUS BIRD,
or, MATESHIP BETRAYED

To some he will seem exemplary:
the frail male lotus bird
balanced uneasily
upon an egg-cradling leaf;
patiently, he will warm all four
to life and precarious flight . . .

His mate, meanwhile—
if that word's not absurd
for an Aussie female bird—
stays just long enough to lay,
flies off to seek for her next clutch
another single dad . . .

63

Their young, some will foresee,
knowing only a broken family,
will mimic parental behaviour—
sexist males will call their sisters flighty
little tarts who always break up the nest.

"HONOUR"

Brown leaves clot the lip of the drain:
the Master paces, chews on his sin;
the girl, compliant serving maid,
tear-flushed beseeches the young man
at the door — who thrusts baffled desire
into the heel of a hand at her throat;
her brother looks on approving as she dies
unresisting, with swollen anxious eyes.

Brown leaves still clot the lip of the drain.

TUTORIAL SUBTEXT, 1951

(A Footnote to Philip Larkin)

They thought her a giggle,
hugely spectacled, tight-strung;
crossing and unwinding
blatant blanched knees,
she smokescreened them out;
talked the tiresome hour down—
freed then to write
or phone her distant one:
they, much deceived, never rumbled,
hazed in their fumbling affaires,
that her life was devoted
to their "best young poet."

HARASSING ENCOUNTER

The small round-faced girl—
among the brightest—
stopped by to regret
she'd been unable
to complete the assignment:
that needed no apology
he smiled, it was optional—
but there was more:
"My Mom has cancer,
she's having chemo."
Suddenly, her eyes filled:
what once he might have ventured
he did not do, but aimed
consoling words across
careful space, mouthed
academic compassion.

65

"TOGETHER AGAIN"

We strolled in the field
of stranded stones and noted
wryly their chill modern declension
from Christian phrases of consolation
to reticent names and dates:
you said — turning in chestnut-filtered
evening light — you wished your ashes
scattered upon the sea . . .
Your ashes!
Suddenly I felt your mouth grate
on mine, your skin puckered and pursed
to the bone. Then
you were yourself and we laughed.

But will you hear what I wish?
No less than those sanguine inscriptions
claim, to be "Together Again."

FOR TROTWOOD

(d. 19 November 1995)

His death concerns only us who loved him
and whom he loved back:
we shall remember
the paws reached soft to our cheek
and the low murmur
when he deserted his chair for a lap:
he would turn and throw himself crosswise
to gaze up with eyes frank enough
to draw us entirely in.

Eight years had made it possible
to believe in his constant presence,
as though he knew how not to die;
death chose a calm bright Sunday
and he was by noon inside
the earth he so often turned.

Each day had ended with a leap to the shoulder
and a purring ride downstairs . . .

No deaths are more important
than mere animals' when they love
without measure or reserve.

A BRIGHT MOMENT

For L.S.

After heavy days the sun broke free,
birds winged with blue flashes
       invested every tree;
       emerging from the shade,
       slow-pacing her garden—
"We buried," she said,"our friend today"
       (it had been nine weeks,
       a great bloodletting stroke)
       and then she smiled,
cracking her pink, velvety cheeks
       (herself not young,
       companion to pain):
       "I wonder what it can be,
       all our friends are dying—
but see, we're somehow alive."

RUN TO EARTH

Piston-armed, tense-chested,
they stride from suburban drives,
tee-shirted and sneakered
in youthful guise,
intent to stretch their lives,
deny loose flesh, mottled skin:
they know they are not old—
it's merely a mask they must wear—
but the young are undeceived,
view them as a species
remote as birds on a wire:
only, when they fly down
in the hard winter of age,
they will feed them,
at touch of their fluttering chests
feel kin,
       glimpse all must run
into time's humus
          in turn. . .